Dutch text 2018 by Corien Oranje
Illustrations 2018 by Marieke ten Berge
This edition copyright © 2020 Lion Hudson IP Limited

Published by
**Lion Hudson Limited**
Wilkinson House, Jordan Hill Business Park
Banbury Road, Oxford OX2 8DR, England
www.lionhudson.com

ISBN 978 0 7459 7846 8

Originally published in Dutch under the title: "Neushoorn en Narwal" by Marieke ten Berge (illustrations) and Corien Oranje (text).

Copyright © 2018 Uitgeverij Columbus, Heerenveen, The Netherlands.

Uitgeverij Columbus is part of Royal Jongbloed Publishers

First English edition 2020

A catalogue record for this book is available from the British Library

Printed and bound in China, November 2019, LH54

# RHINO
## AND
# NARWHAL

## ANIMAL HIDE AND SEEK

*Based on words by* **Corien Oranje**

*Illustrated by* **Marieke ten Berge**

**LION**
CHILDREN'S

CAN YOU FIND THE RHINO AND THE NARWHAL ON EACH PAGE?

HINT: ONLY PARTS OF THEM MAY BE SEEN.

LOOK OUT FOR THE BOY WITH DARK CURLS

AND THE GIRL WITH BLONDE HAIR, TOO.

# CONTENTS

# IN THE JUNGLE

The jungle has many trees and other plants. Hiding among the leaves and branches are birds, insects, and other animals. Which ones do you know?

- *Can you find the toucans, the sloth, and the ring-tailed lemurs?*
- *How many monkeys can you find?*
- *Where is the baby koala hiding?*
- *God gave the python a skin that is perfect for hiding. Do you see it?*

*• Answer: There are four monkeys.*

# SNOW AND ICE

In the lands of ice and snow, animals can survive the cold. The polar bears and the yak have thick coats of fur. The humpback whale and the leopard seals have thick layers of blubber.

- *How many penguins can you find?*
- *Do you see the snowy owl and the arctic fox?*
- *Where did the moose go?*
- *What baby animals can you see?*

- *Answer: There are ten penguins.*

# FAST AND SLOW

Animals can move in many different ways. Some fly, some leap, some hop, some crawl, and some gallop. Which ones can you name?

- *White-throated needletails are some of the fastest birds. Can you see them?*
- *Can you find the jumping mouse? It can jump more than the length of a bed.*
- *Do you see the spotty cheetah, the fastest land animal?*
- *Which animal did God give a shell to hide in?*

• Answer: The snail.

# TEENY TINY CREEPY CRAWLIES

Insects are the largest group of animals. They buzz, fly, and scuttle from plant to plant. Which ones do you know?

- *Do you know what insect comes out of the caterpillar's cocoon?*
- *Where is the stag beetle hiding?*
- *Do you see the moth? It has big black eyes.*
- *Can you find the honeybee?*

*• Answer: A butterfly comes out of the cocoon.*

# UNDER THE GROUND

Some animals make their homes under the ground. They dig out tunnels leading to their burrows. There they sleep safely and keep warm.

- *Can you help the mole get to the key and treasure chest?*
- *Where did the squirrel hide its glass jar with nuts?*
- *The badger's home is called a sett. Can you find it?*
- *Long ago, God also created dinosaurs! Can you find the bones of a dinosaur's tail?*

# SMOOTH AND HAIRY

Mammals have fluffy fur. Reptiles have smooth scales or shells. Amphibians have slimy skin. They may be covered in zig-zags, spots, or stripes. What different patterns can you see?

- *Can you find the porcupine with its sharp spines?*
- *Will you help the little okapis find their mother? They all have the same stripes.*
- *God gave the armadillo a bony shell over its fur. Can you find it?*

# UP IN THE AIR

Birds fill the skies, swooping, soaring, flapping, and gliding. A group of birds is called a flock. Many birds fly a long way every year. Which ones do you know?

• *Can you find the white dove, the puffin, and the eagle?*
• *The hummingbird has a thin pointy beak. Where is it hiding?*
• *God has given the bird of paradise splendid feathers. Can you find it?*

# UNDER WATER

The oceans are full of animals. Fish swim in a group called a shoal. Whales and other animals dive down deep. Which ones can you name?

- *How many sea turtles can you see?*
- *Where are the manta ray, the hammerhead shark, and the squid?*
- *The walrus has long tusks. Can you find it?*
- *Do you see the pufferfish? It looks like a balloon.*

• *Answer: There are four sea turtles.*

## AT NIGHT

Some animals are awake at night. Many have large eyes to see in the dark. Others can smell very well. God created the moon and stars to give some light.

• *The baby quokka is hiding in its mother's pouch. Can you find it?*
• *Do you know where the elephant shrew is?*
• *Do you see the grey mouse lemur with its giant eyes?*
• *Can you howl like a wolf and hoot like an owl?*

# ANIMAL BABIES

Mother animals care for their babies. Mothers feed their young, and help them until they have grown. God gave all animals a mother, including you and me.

- *A baby swan is called a cygnet. Can you find it?*
- *Where is the baby tapir with its mother?*
- *Can you see mother elephant's trunk?*
- *The baby sea otter can't swim so it lies on its mother's tummy. Can you find them?*

ARCTIC FOX

ARMADILLO

BADGER

BIRD OF PARADISE

BUTTERFLY

CATERPILLAR COCOON

CHEETAH

DINOSAUR BONES

DOVE

EAGLE

ELEPHANT

ELEPHANT SHREW

GREY MOUSE LEMUR

HAMMERHEAD SHARK

HONEYBEE

HUMMINGBIRD

HUMPBACK WHALE

JUMPING MOUSE

KOALA

LEOPARD SEAL

MANTA RAY

MOLE

MONKEY

MOOSE

MOTH

OKAPI

OWL

PENGUIN

POLAR BEAR

PORCUPINE

PUFFERFISH

PUFFIN

PYTHON

QUOKKA

RING—TAILED
LEMUR

SEA OTTER

SEA TURTLE